SCAVENGERS

WRITTEN AND ILLUSTRATED BY

OLIVE L. EARLE

William Morrow and Company   New York 1973

Earle, Olive Lydia.
    Scavengers.

    SUMMARY: Introduces the physical characteristics and
habits of various scavenger insects, birds, and other
animals that clean up waste materials in their environment.
    1. Scavengers (Zoology)—Juvenile literature.
[1. Scavengers (Zoology)] I. Title.
QL756.5.E17   591.5′2′4   72–3799
ISBN 0-688-20034-6
ISBN 0-688-30034-0 (lib. bdg.)

Some members of the animal kingdom are known as scavengers, because they clean up filth. By eating it, they rid their environment of the leftovers of a predator's feast, or they eat the carcasses of animals and birds that have died a natural death. Most are not fussy about the freshness of their food, for apparently they enjoy putrid meat. Some eat decayed plants. Others eat dung; such droppings, called feces, are made up of digested material and may provide nutrients lacking in the eater's diet.

While the habits of scavengers may seem revolting to us, without them the world would become littered with decayed material. These animals and birds perform very valuable services, for they are the garbage collectors of nature's sanitation department.

Small and large scavengers, from maggots to big animals, all do their particular

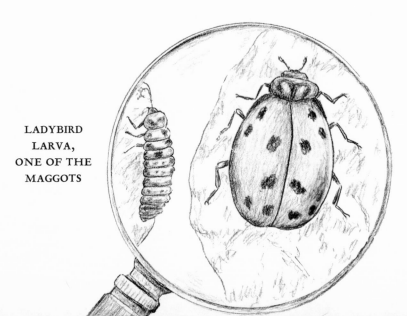

LADYBIRD LARVA, ONE OF THE MAGGOTS

ADULT LADYBIRD

kind of service. Even the common earth-worm does its share of improving its territory. Because the worm discharges the waste from the decayed plant and animal material it has eaten, the soil is ultimately enriched. When it is digging its burrow, the worm swallows some of the earth through which it is tunneling. This soil, together with the food it has nipped off with its extended upper lip, is digested and pulverized; the nourishing parts are absorbed, and the residue is ejected through an opening at the tip of the pointed tail. This waste matter can be seen near a burrow's doorway. It is in the form of small coiled mounds called castings. These castings make such valuable soil that sometimes they are collected by gardeners for use when potting house plants.

In addition to creating rich soil, the earthworm distributes needed air to the roots of plants by its burrowing. The tunnels may be from six inches to several feet below the surface of the ground; they act as ducts for the rainwater required by most plants, channeling moisture to the roots.

Worms are active on the soil's surface

at night, for even though they have no eyes, they are sensitive to bright light and avoid it. Fishermen, who sometimes collect large worms for use as bait, call them "night crawlers." In the tropics there are giant earthworms that may stretch to a length of over five feet, but elsewhere species are smaller. Fully grown, common earthworms may be from six to twelve inches long.

Though earthworms flourish in damp ground, a heavy rain may wash them out of their burrows or even drown them in their tunnels. A worm dies if it is stranded on a concrete walk or a large stone and cannot get back to its old burrow or is unable to dig a new one.

But even a dead worm is useful, because it provides scavenging ants with a feast. A number of these insects, pushing and pulling, drag the prize to their nest for the benefit of the colony. The busy ants find their way back to their retreat by following the trail of odor left when they emerged from it.

The so-called white ants are not true ants, but are termites. In tropical areas, termites build huge earthen mounds for their headquarters. Species native to cooler regions inhabit galleries they have eaten in wood. With the help of minute one-

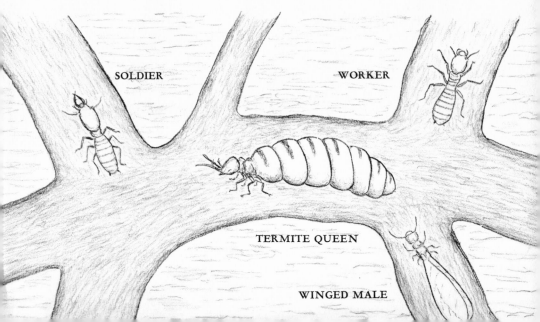

celled animals that live in their digestive tracts, they are able to consume the tough wood fibers. Often these termites seem to be man's enemies, for they may invade the woodwork of houses and, tunneling unseen, destroy it. But colonies of termites are useful when they reduce to pulp the slowly rotting wood of fallen trees. Forests might be cluttered with dead tree trunks and branches without the work of communities of hard-working termites.

TROPICAL
TERMITE
MOUND

SOLDIER

WORKER

TERMITE QUEEN

WINGED MALE

Some of the almost innumerable kinds of beetles are also famous for how they improve their territory. The burying, or sexton, beetle is one such insect. Beetles of this group bury small dead creatures such as little birds, mice, moles, frogs, and small snakes. In this way they clean up the environment.

The burying beetle is thought to have a good sense of smell, for it quickly finds anything that has died in its neighborhood. On discovering a corpse, the beetle seems

able to communicate with others some distance away. Soon several helpers arrive to assist with the interment of the body. To bury a corpse so much bigger than themselves, the insects use their claws to dig the earth from beneath it. The carcass sinks lower and lower into its grave while the excavated earth banks up around it. This earth slides back on top of the body and, at last, completely covers it.

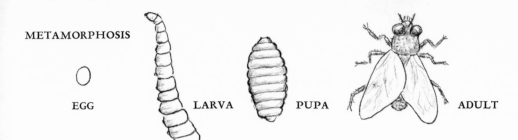

METAMORPHOSIS

EGG   LARVA   PUPA   ADULT

BEETLE
LARVA

A female beetle often lays her eggs in the carcass. The flesh decays and provides soft food for the larvae (grubs) when they hatch from the eggs. Undergoing metamorphosis, as it is called, a larva becomes a pupa (the nonfeeding stage of development), and from the pupa a young beetle eventually emerges.

The largest of the North American sexton beetles is almost one and one-half inches long. Its general color is black. There are two red spots or bands on the stiff front wings that shield the more fragile pair of wings beneath them.

In the huge scarab family of beetles, there are also species that clean up their surroundings. A number of them are admired for their brilliant colors, and in some places the dried insect, used like a jewel, is mounted in rings and brooches. In ancient Egypt a scarab known as a dung beetle was considered a sacred symbol. The ball of dung associated with the insect represented the earth; the beetle represented the sun. Drawings of the insects appear on tombs, and gem stones were carved in their likeness.

Actually dung beetles are useful in a less decorative way for they are energetic removers of animal waste. One may operate alone, or a pair may work as a team. The beetles roll a compact ball made from scraps of animal droppings to a burrow and deposit it there. This activity earns the insect the name of tumble bug. The dung beetle lays its eggs in the pellet, and the decayed vegetable matter in it becomes food for the developing young. The life cycle is similar to that of the burying beetle.

Among the mammals, there are helpful scavengers too. The Virginia opossum is one, for it will eat anything available, decayed or fresh. It has a bad reputation, because it may steal chickens or eggs. This hen-house raiding cannot be denied, but possibly a big rat or a weasel may be guilty of some of the thievery blamed on the opossum. Because the opossum is slow in its movements, it usually fails to catch a wild bird, but on its nightly rambles it eats any dead one that it finds. Also it enjoys a meal of snake, mouse, fruit, or insects.

Having spread from its southern range, the Virginia opossum is now at home in the wooded suburbs of Northern cities. There, as it waddles along, it may find an overturned garbage container. This prize can provide it with a ready-made feast of animal and vegetable discards.

With short legs, and a body about the

size of a large cat, the Virginia opossum wears a bushy coat of blackish and brownish coarse hair intermixed with white. Its naked tail is prehensile, for it can be wrapped around a small branch and used as a safety device when the animal is on a tree-climbing expedition. The opossum is famous for its trick of playing dead. It flops over, seemingly lifeless, when it is frightened. When the danger passes, it trots away.

Another scavenger whose home is farther north than that of the opossum is the fisher. Having been exterminated by continuous hunting in more southerly areas where once it lived, it now is found only in Northern states and in Canada. The name fisher is somewhat misleading, for it does not catch live fish. Instead it cleans up the dead ones it finds along the shores of lakes and rivers. In fact, the fisher dines on anything available, from dead animals caught in traps to whatever it can

catch for itself. At times it climbs trees for a meal of fruit or nuts.

Somewhat foxlike in appearance, the fisher is the largest member of the weasel family except for the wolverine. Chiefly dark brown in color, its body may be about thirty inches in length, and its tail about fifteen inches long. Trappers seek the fisher for its rare beautiful pelt and sell the furs to people who make them into coats for those who like to wear the skins of dead animals.

As the name suggests, the Arctic fox lives farther north than the fisher. Its sanitation work consists of clearing up the remnants of a polar bear's meal of seal meat. A grouse known as the ptarmigan is another favorite food of this fox. Sometimes it digs the bird from its shelter burrowed in a snowbank. But the ice floes are the surest place for the fox to find food. There it can scavenge leftover seal meat or dine on a polar bear's feces. In the summer, the Arctic fox may catch lemmings. These somewhat mouselike, short-tailed rodents are famous for their periodic

migrations that take place when their territory becomes overpopulated.

The Arctic fox is smaller, has a less pointed muzzle, and rounder ears than the better-known American red fox of more southerly areas. In the summer, the coat of the Arctic fox becomes bluish or bluish brown and is less furry than the white one it wears in winter. In some parts of its

AMERICAN RED FOX

range no color change occurs or it is in-
complete; then the animal is called a blue
fox. Fur buyers consider the blue color
phase desirable, and the fox is hunted for
its valuable pelt. If the trapper stopped to
think, he would realize that the skin is
more valuable to the fox than to anyone
else.

Wolves are closely related to foxes, for

GRAY WOLF

both are members of the dog family, and they too are scavengers. The gray, or timber, wolf sometimes weighs as much as one hundred and seventy pounds and once ranged all over North America. Three hundred years ago there were so many of them that a dead wolf was worth very little in bounty money. At that time, one penny was the reward paid for killing a wolf. The animals were hated, because they hunted in packs and attacked farm livestock. Today timber wolves are almost extinct south of the Canadian border.

Poisoned carcasses, set out as bait, have
been fatal to them. Normally they devour
carrion and bring swift death to ailing
deer and other animals.

There are wolves in captivity, and many
of them have become as tame and friendly
as a pet dog. Numbers of people are inter-
ested in wolves and enjoy the sound of
their howls by listening to recordings
made of a wolf chorus.

The prairie wolf, commonly known as the coyote (ki-o'te or ki'ot) pays with its life when it scavenges a poisoned carcass. Humane people are trying to prevent the killing of these useful animals. Roaming pet dogs have died from eating poisoned bait intended for coyotes, and this possibility has increased the outcry against its use. Coyotes are now protected on Federal lands, and, despite efforts to exterminate them elsewhere, they seem to be holding their own in many Western regions.

Though a coyote may occasionally attack a sheep or a lamb, it plays its part in the balance of nature by devouring dead animals. It also destroys rats, mice, jackrabbits, and ground squirrels. When not kept in check by coyotes, these animals can become pests and ruin the grain crops and the grazing areas needed for a rancher's animals.

The coyote's voice, usually heard at

night, is a wailing yelp mixed with a sharp bark. About the size of a small police dog, the coyote has a yellowish-gray coat. Unlike a running gray wolf's tail, which usually stretches out like a flag in the breeze, the coyote's tail generally droops downward as it trots along. The female bears four or more pups. Young animals are easily tamed and make good pets.

No bigger than the coyote, the jackal of the Old World is another scavenger in the dog tribe. It is one of the most notorious, for it has been known to dig up and devour human bodies that have been buried in shallow graves.

The Asian jackal is somewhat smaller than the African variety. The latter are renowned for their ability to get a share of zebra or some other animal killed by lions.

A pack of jackals may wait until the sur-
feited lions have wandered away. They are
so agile, however, that they sometimes
dart in among the eating lions and fear-
lessly grab a mouthful of meat.

From their dens among rocks, usually

under cover of darkness, jackals may
emerge to do their own killing. At times
they run down a small antelope or catch
the straying young of larger animals.
Jackals dine on all kinds of food, for besides devouring fresh and decayed meat,

they eat a certain amount of plant matter. Some of it may be obtained at second hand, as when they eat the dung of the vegetarian rhinoceros. In the feces are the remains of green food the rhinoceros has eaten.

In parts of Africa, the jackals' territory is often shared by packs of hyenas, who have similar carrion-eating habits. Hyenas clean up the abandoned remains of a lion's kill or dine on any and every dead animal that they find. Undoubtedly, they are among the top-ranking collectors of offal. Hyenas are larger in size than jackals and, when they hunt their own meals, may

tackle a wildebeest or any animal that is not too big or too swift.

The hyena is noted for having the strongest jaws of all the meat eaters and is able to crunch and eat big bones. Because the animal's front legs are longer than the hind ones, its back has a peculiar slope. This design gives it an awkward, shambling gait, but it is able to run at a good pace when the need arises.

The name of laughing hyena is given the animal, because it makes whooping cries that sound like shrieks of human laughter. It also barks and growls.

Throughout the world there are a great many birds who are sanitation experts. Some of them live in the same general regions as the hyenas and the jackals. One such scavenging bird is the marabou, or marabou stork. Its carrion-eating habits set it apart from other storks who ordinarily catch and eat a variety of live food. Because it is such a good garbage collector, the marabou is protected by law in numerous places.

WHITE STORK
WITH LIVE FOOD

This stork, standing about four feet tall, is sometimes known as the adjutant bird. It gets this name because of the soldierly precision with which it strides about on its long legs. The bird's heavy

MARABOUS AND
EGYPTIAN VULTURE

bill is straight and pointed; as a weapon it is so effective that other scavengers are likely to give the marabou first claim to a carcass. The bird also eats any small animals that it can catch.

The plumage of this stork's back is a dark metallic green, and the shaggy feathers on its underparts are white. In the breeding season, fluffy feathers grow in the region of the tail. At one time, they were used extensively for the trimming of ladies' hats and dresses. A few downy or hairy feathers adorn the bird's otherwise naked, reddish head and neck. Many scavenging birds have a bare or partly bare head and neck. This provision of nature is useful, for feathers soon would

become messy from meals. From the marabou's throat, there hangs a strange sausage-like pouch, which may be a foot or so long; its use to the bird is not fully understood.

In the same regions with the marabous are species of vultures. These scavenging birds give other garbage collectors notice of the whereabouts of feasting lions by swooping down from the sky. Vultures have extremely keen eyesight, and possibly they also can smell the presence of a dead animal.

The eared, or sociable, vulture is one such guide. Flocks of these birds gather to finish the remains of meals left by lions or other predators. For the tearing of flesh, the bird has a hook at the tip of its straight beak. The eared vulture's feet are not so strong as those of many birds of prey. It does not carry food in its claws to its sitting mate or hatched young, but disgorges at the nest some of the meat it has swallowed. It is a very large bird measuring forty to forty-five inches from tail end to the tip of its beak.

The much smaller Egyptian vulture is about twenty-four inches in length. It is another useful scavenging bird, which differs from many of its kind because the head and neck, except for its bare face, are feathered. The adults are mainly whitish, while the juvenile birds have brown plumage. Flocks of these vultures descend on any animal corpse to devour it. The birds also are known to break and eat the contents of eggs laid by a ground-nesting bird such as the ostrich. Because this vulture often appears in ancient Egyptian drawings, it is sometimes called Pharoah's chicken.

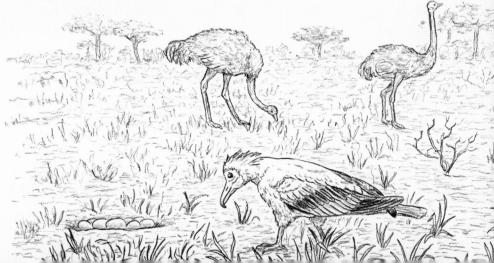

There are many species of vultures living in various parts of the world. The prize for size, however, goes to the condors. The Andean condor has a wingspread of from nine to ten feet; it is one of the largest flying birds. These South American vultures are at home in almost the entire range of the Andes Mountains. A dead llama or any other available carrion is food for them. They may travel to the edge of the sea to hunt for a dead whale or other marine animals that have been

washed ashore. The birds soar magnificently, but have difficulty in flying up from the ground when gorged with food.

The male Andean condor's bare, pinkish head is ornamented with a fleshy crest over its eyes and above the base of its hooked beak. Around its neck the bird wears a collar of fluffy white feathers. The general color of the plumage is glossy black, with some gray on the wings.

The California condor is almost as big as its Andean relative. It is about the most threatened on the list of vanishing species in the United States, for it is thought that only forty or so of the birds are alive today.

These rarities live in an almost inaccessible coastal mountain range, but at times they fly to areas where they may eat a carcass poisoned by ranchers. The female lays a single egg at nesting time, and it is believed that she nests only every second year. This condor's plumage is mainly black; its bare head is yellowish orange and red.

A featherless red head is a characteristic of the brownish turkey vulture. In many places this bird is commonly called a "buzzard." It ranges from North to South America and is a valuable gatherer of trash wherever it sets up housekeeping. Man's presence usually means careless disposal of waste materials that may contain a meal for a buzzard. Ever on the lookout, the birds occasionally are seen on the roof of a city building. They also walk around village gardens looking for anything edible.

When the thirty-inch-long bird is on a hunting expedition, it soars on outstretched wings for hour after hour. It flies in circles, turning its head from side to side, so that its keen eyes will not miss a possible meal. When a feast comes into view, the bird swoops down and is followed quickly by others of its kind. Together, they gorge until they can eat no more. The turkey vulture favors decayed flesh, perhaps that of an alligator. If no carrion is available, and garbage is scarce, it dines on snakes, toads, and small mammals such as mice.

The bald eagle is also a refuse collector
and is especially fond of eating dead fish.
Sometimes no such meal is ready and wait-
ing at the seashore or at the edge of a lake.
Then the bird becomes a pirate. It will
bully a fish hawk (osprey) that is flying

to a perch with a freshly caught fish in its claws. The eagle dives repeatedly at the osprey until the tormented bird drops the fish. Then the robber grabs the loot. Besides dining on seafood, the bald eagle will eat any dead animal it comes across. A duck, wounded by a hunter, may be put out of its misery by the foraging bird.

The head of an adult bald eagle is white, as are its tail feathers; its remaining

plumage is dark brown. Young birds do not have this typical plumage until their fourth year. The female, thirty-six inches long, is rather larger than the male.

Bald eagles, though protected by law since 1940, are decreasing in numbers. This decline may be the result of man's cutting down trees that were favored nesting sites. Or it may be caused by the use of pesticides whose poison has reached

BALD EAGLE

IMMATURE
BALD EAGLE

GOLDEN EAGLE

the fish eaten by eagles with fatal results.

Sometimes a young bald eagle is mistaken for a golden eagle and shot. Now, however, golden eagles also are protected. They, too, include carrion in their diet.

Among the many birds that are diligent collectors of trash are the numerous species of gulls. Water is a favored source of food for them. One is the common, or herring, gull. It is at home along the seacoast and near the shores of inland waters. It also is the bird most frequently seen following ships far out to sea. There it picks up the edible refuse thrown overboard from a ship's galley. Huge flocks of these gulls, with mewing calls, invade man's garbage dumps and gobble up everything they can eat, no matter how decayed. They haunt places where fishermen are cleaning their catch and enjoy the rubbish left on a beach by messy picnickers. At times they make trips inland to feast on berries and other vegetable food. They eat grasshoppers and will follow a plough to collect worms and insects from the upturned earth.

The herring gull drinks either fresh or salt water. Like many marine birds, the gull has a pair of glands near the eyes for the concentration of the salt in seawater. The salt drains out through slits in the bird's bill.

Common sea gulls are famous for the manner in which they get the meat out of a closed clamshell. On a sand flat, the bird may find a clam and, carrying the prize in its bill, fly to a height of some forty feet above a rock or paved road. Then it drops the clam, and the shell breaks on the

hard surface. The bird dives down to eat the exposed insides. Occasionally a watching crow darts down to grab the clam meat before the gull can reach it.

The gull is a master of skillful flight. Birds in a huge flock hardly ever collide. Using their feet as rudders, they steer away from each other even when several swoop down to snatch the same floating fragment. Often they follow a ship without any movement of their outstretched wings, expertly riding the currents of air

sent upward by the movement of the water at the ship's stern. They swim well, their pinkish feet acting as paddles. The three front toes are webbed, but the rear toe is only partly developed.

The herring gull's plumage alters in color as the bird ages. A young bird is mostly brownish, and it does not assume adult coloration until it is three years old. At that time it has reached a length of twenty-four inches and is mostly white with a grayish blue mantle. The long, black-tipped wing feathers have white markings.

JUVENILE

NESTLING

Related to the gulls are the seabirds known as either skuas or jaegers (ya′gers). The great skua is brown in general color and is about the size of a herring gull. This scavenging bird is at home in both South and North Pole regions and, being a wanderer, occasionally may appear in warmer latitudes.

Skuas follow ships to pick up any offal thrown overboard. They bully other birds into disgorging their food and catch it as it falls. By stealing eggs or killing young birds who have wandered too far from a protecting parent, they help control the population of penguins and other ground-nesting birds. They also eat small mammals and devour any carrion that they find.

The only resident scavenger of Antarctica is said to be the common sheathbill. It also is a bird that preys on penguins, stealing their eggs and young and devouring the bodies of dead adults. While it does eat some seaweeds, its main food is offal of all sorts—from carcasses to the feces of penguins and seals. As yet unafraid of man, small flocks of the birds collect edible garbage from whaling stations and outposts of science expeditions.

The name sheathbill is given the bird

because of the horny sheath that covers
the base of its short, heavy bill. On ac-
count of the featherless, somewhat warty
pink skin around its eyes, sailors sometimes
call the bird "sore-eyed pigeon." About
seventeen inches in length, the sheathbill is not unlike a rather large domestic
pigeon in shape. The plumage is entirely
white, the legs are bluish gray. While
most shorebirds have webbed feet, the
sheathbill does not.

A famous scavenging seabird is the wandering albatross. Widely distributed throughout Southern oceans, it is the largest member of the albatross family. This ship follower is renowned for its long-distance flying and is ever on the watch for a whaling vessel from which chunks of blubber may be discarded. If it finds no such satisfying waste, the bird contents itself with meals of squid, jelly-fish, and other sea creatures that may be churned to the surface by the ship's pro-pellers.

When there is no ship to help it get its food, the albatross dines on any floating animal matter it can find. The bird does not dive below the water's surface to feed, even though its webbed feet propel it well through the waves. It also is able to run on top of the water; it may travel as far as seventy yards on the surface in order to gain the momentum necessary to launch itself into the air.

The big wandering albatross has white plumage except for the black feathers in its long wings, which have a span of over eleven feet. Traveling on these wings, out-stretched and motionless in flight, the bird takes advantage of air currents and glides effortlessly for miles.

Except in the breeding season, wander-ing albatrosses seldom visit land. Their short legs, set far back under their heavy bodies, make taking off from the ground difficult. As members of a colony on a remote island, a pair become parents once every two years and then have only one downy chick. The baby bird hatches from

an egg that was laid on bare ground some seventy-three days earlier.

The harsh, croaking voice of the albatross is somewhat similar to the most frequent call given by another refuse collector, the common raven. This land bird occasionally adds grunts and screams to its usual croaks. The twenty-seven-inch-long common raven is the largest member of the crow family, many of whom are scavengers to some degree.

FISH CROW

This raven is at home mainly in the Northwestern states, where it ordinarily lives in isolated rocky areas of mountainous country. But sometimes a flock of the birds seek out places where people live, for the sake of getting easy meals from the garbage. They are not particular about the freshness of their food. Any dead animal is on their menu, and they eat fruit and nuts as well. In the far North, the raven and the Arctic fox share leftovers from the kill of a polar bear. At the edge of open water, these birds sometimes are lucky and find a dead fish.

RAVEN

People use the word *raven* to describe a rich black color. Yet they may not realize that the term is borrowed from the purple-glossed black plumage of the handsome scavenger. The female's plumage is a less lustrous black.

Common ravens are thought to mate for life and, year after year, are likely to return to the same nesting area. High on a cliff, a nest is built of interlaced sticks lined with coarse grass. Near the seashore, seaweed may be used to form a cushion for six or seven eggs. Sometimes a young raven is captured and kept as a pet. Easily

tamed and intelligent, the bird is full of mischief and delights in stealing and hiding glittering objects.

Besides the well-known scavengers, there are many part-time garbage collectors. Numerous animals and birds eat carrion when their normal food is not available because of bad weather or other un-favorable conditions. Like a hungry person, a starving animal is not fussy about its food. Whether full-time or part-time, scavengers show us that cleaning up the environment is a good thing to do.

INDEX

indicates illustrations